SOMEWHERE IN IRELAND

Somewhere in Ireland

A JOURNEY OF DISCOVERY

poems by
Linda Whittenberg

artwork by
Lillie Morris

Copyright © 2011 by Linda Whittenberg.
All rights reserved.
First Edition

Artwork by Lillie Morris
including cover art: "Thinking of Ireland" and
"*Biseanna, Clocha, agus Tui* (Spirals, Stones and Straw)"

* * *

Book Design by Marsha Ahrenkiel
Black Swan Editions logo by Steve Counsell

No part of this book may be reproduced in any form or by any electronic or mechanical means including information storage and retrieval systems without permission in writing from the publisher, except by a reviewer who may quote brief passages in a review.

Library of Congress Cataloging-in-Publication Data
Whittenberg, Linda, 1937 -
Somewhere in Ireland: poems / by Linda Whittenberg

ISBN 978-0-9825156-1-7

Copies may be purchased at
www.lindawhittenberg.com

Other works by Linda Whittenberg

Dying Can Wait

Tender Harvest

To the Memory of My Grandfather

William Michael Shannon
(1883-1971)

From country music to cards, gardening to whittling, checkers to chickens, my grandfather gave me what he had to give. He taught me how to pick a winning racehorse, the superior qualities of mules, and appreciation for honest hard work. His stories delighted my young mind, planting the seeds that made a storyteller of me. Once, when I accidentally inhaled a small harmonica part and couldn't breathe, he lifted me by the heels and slapped my back, sending the harmonica part flying. Just as surely as that heroic gesture saved my life, his love blessed me for all the years to come. It is my enduring admiration and love for him that inspires my interest in the land of our ancestors.

Preface

When my husband and I travelled to Ireland to attend Writers' Week 2010 in Listowel, County Kerry, a remarkable journey began. It was as if the land itself were saying: *Welcome, Daughter, stories, images, fantasies await you. Enjoy, embrace, feast, and learn. We've been waiting for you. Céad míle fáilte (kad meel-a fall-sha), a hundred thousand welcomes.*

Questions presented themselves at every turn: What does it mean to be Irish? What aspects of my personality, imagination, character come from that side of my heritage? Who were the Shannons? Where did they live? What was it like for those who stayed, for those who left? From where does the deep longing come? How does one explain the feeling of familiarity so strong, at times, it feels more like memory than imagining?

It is my hope the poems and prose in *Somewhere in Ireland* will speak to others who long for places of deep, soulful connection, especially to those who have traveled to Ireland and made discoveries of their own.

In many ways this book is a sequel to my earlier book *Tender Harvest.* Many of the poems in that collection were written in appreciation of my forbearers. *Somewhere in Ireland* pays special tribute to my grandfather, Will Shannon, who was one of the most significant figures in my young life.

Many attributes I admired in Grandfather, I believe came from his Irish heritage; yet, he himself never had the opportunity to travel to Ireland. Now, with this book, a circle has been completed.

The Michael Shannons

My great-great-grandfather, Michael Shannon, sailed from Liverpool to New York Harbor in 1849 during the Great Famine. Although information about him is scarce, the U.S. Census lists him as being born in Ireland in 1825 and as *farmer*, living in New Haven, Connecticut in the 1850s. His son, also Michael Shannon, my great-grandfather, born in 1851, spent his adult years in rural Illinois, married twice and had two sons, Edward and William Michael, my grandfather.

According to family stories, Michael Shannon, my great-grandfather, was an alcoholic of the worst kind. One night in 1888 when he had been out drinking, he didn't make it home. Some have conjectured my great-grandmother Louisa may have had her brothers do him in. Others thought, coming home late at night, he may have crossed a neighbor's land and been shot. His death was never investigated nor satisfactorily explained.

Since there are a number of Michael Shannons in these poems, I have attempted to make it clear which person I'm referring to: Michael Shannon, my great-great-grandfather, who emigrated; his son, Michael Shannon, my great-grandfather; or Michaél Shannon, a current-day citizen of Doolin, County Clare, keeper of Shannon history, storyteller, and friend. As far as we know, I am not related to Michaél; however, considering the people of early Ireland were tribal people, divided into clans, there is a possibility, if we were able to go back far enough, we would find we are related.

CONTENTS

Preface 8

The Michael Shannons 9

Across Wide Waters 15

If You Hadn't Left Ireland So Young

Small Farmers 19

Pentimento 20

On a Day Like Today 23

Escape 24

Noel O'Donoghue's Flute 26

You Could Have Been One 27

Bank Holiday Blues 28

Irish Diaspora 29

A Journey of Discovery

Curry for Lunch 33

Tony's Story 34

Sent Off with Prayers 35

Presence 36

I Seem to Remember 38

Providence 39

Crossing to County Clare

The Tarbert Ferry 43

Leprechauns and Fairies at Work 44

It Depends on What You Mean by *True* 47

Michaél Shannon of Doolin, County Clare 48

Celtic Roots 49

Woman by the Sea 50

Close Call 52

Driving on the Wrong Side of the Road 53

Western Shores

Moody Lion 57

Changelings 58

The Great Tree, *Crann Bethadh* 59

Huntress 60

Early Morning Belongs to Cows and Crows 61

The Town Donkey 62

Ruminations on Cows 63

Along the Craggy Shore 64

Haunted 67

The People of County Clare

Brief Encounter ... 71

Friday Night at Fitzpatrick's ... 72

Word Music ... 74

Milking Time in Winter ... 77

Whittling the Day Away ... 78

Night Coming On ... 79

Educating Bobby O'Connell ... 80

Irish in America

"Farmed Out" ... 85

Beloved ... 86

A Snake Still Lives in Ireland ... 89

Martha Louisa McKinney Shannon ... 90

Men in Gray Suits and Hats ... 92

Grandfather at 50 ... 94

Lunch Time for a Gandy Dancer ... 96

Mining for Coal ... 98

Inheritance ... 100

What's in a Name? ... 101

POSTSCRIPT

Someone's Always Saying Goodbye.................... 104

∞

ARTWORK

Earrach in Éirinn (Springtime in Ireland).............. 21

Western Shores 22

Thinking of Ireland 45

Close to the Edge 46

Beneath the Surface 65

Sara's Piece 66

Fiddle Abstract 75

On the Edge 76

Scriofa i Rúnda (Written in Secret) 87

Irish in America 88

Across Wide Waters

Late in life, you venture to the green land
of your progenitors and enter a story
told in faces of its people,
sounds of its language, its music,
shape of its hills.
Memory of something in you that would have been lost
had you not opened the door, heard a voice saying,
Come in.

If You Hadn't Left Ireland So Young

"To hell or to Connaught"—

In 1652, after ruthlessly putting down one of many Irish rebellions against Protestant English oppression, Cromwell swore the bitter words, *To hell or to Connaught,* words that slashed yet another tear into the fabric of Catholic Irish Society. His meaning was clear: Move to the barren lands of western Ireland or be killed. By 1655, land owned by non-Irish had increased to 75%. In spite of all these hardships and humiliations, an Irish nation still existed—separate, populous, and hostile.

Small Farmers

More likely than not, my ancestors
were among those
squeezed onto rocky knolls
and soggy bogs of western Ireland.

It took stamina, hardiness,
strong faith to endure
two cruel masters,
the English and harsh weather.

From these hardscrabble people,
my grandfather must have inherited the trait
of taking on any kind of hard labor
if it put food on the table.

The women, my aunts and my grandmothers,
could stretch a few potatoes, a bone of lamb,
for a long tableful of men and youngsters.

Fathers and sons old enough
toted, hoisted, chinked and cleared,
for the land was either rock or mud,
depending on luck of the draw.

With maybe one cow, turf for fires,
a plot of potatoes, they kept at it,
paying high rent for the privilege
of living on the edge of disaster.

Pentimento*

Green pastures, amber fields
sweep across valleys and hills,
hectares defined by stone walls,
keeping one man's cows from
another man's clover.

So beguiling this landscape,
easy to miss the shadow images
beneath the vibrant color.
A pentimento,
life nearly squeezed out of the
people whose crime was being Irish.

Layer upon layer of rural charm
painted over—
fierce rebellions and wars,
blighted crops, penal laws.
The struggles bleed through
only if you look close enough.

Stone upon stone
like broken granite lace,**
embellishing a landscape
so sublime one could forget,
so lovely it wrenches the heart.

* *Pentimento—*
  The presence of earlier images painted over.

** *You'd swear the hills were edged with broken granite lace . . .*
  from "These Dry Stone Walls"
  Song by DAVE GOULDER

Earrach in Éirinn (Springtime in Ireland)
Mixed Media Collage

Western Shores
Mixed Media Collage

On a Day Like Today

On the day you embarked,
Michael Shannon, was it like today—
no wind, sunlight bouncing off the water,
green laid out over the hills?
Were the islands distinct that day,
gray stone against blue sky?

If it were a day like today when you left,
surely the image must have stayed with you
'til the end of your days.
Surely, you had no other choice
or you would never have been able
to leave for Cork, Cobh Harbor,
the wharf, the ship
that would take you from here.

Escape

That last day in Ireland—
       with everything gone
       except a few ragged clothes in a duffle,
I made it to the dock early to queue up
for passage to America.

I was used to waiting at the agency window.
In line for hours, we waited,
       all of us brought down to skin over bone,
       all of us praying for any offer of labor,
no matter how loathsome.

When blight took our home, our land,
       my family, like others
       who couldn't make the rent,
set up in a ditch, squatting
on a few miserable square meters
with only a scrap of canvas for shelter.

Just down the oak-lined lane
the Big House stood empty,
       its owners enjoying
       the good life in London or Bath,
leaving an Irish overseer who was meaner yet
when it came to handing down mercy.

Landowners wanted no part of sunken-eyed beggars
scratching at their doors,
>   the fever,
>   the stench,
bodies piling up faster than they could be buried.

Let me tell you how it was that last day—
nostalgia, no; anger and savage hunger,
>   the kind that makes you do
>   what you never thought you would,
anything for food,
things that could cause you
never to feel good again.

Noel O'Donoghue's Flute

His flute plays the tunes
you whistled as a lad.
He starts up with a feisty jig
you used to dance to,
the kind of tune that only comes back
after your belly is full and
hunger has subsided.

He knows the one that doodled
in the back of your head
as you clung to the ship's rail,
wind flapping your coattails.
An air that always reminded
you of home.

I may never know:
Did you take the government pay-off,
you, like so many others?
Did a charity pay your passage?
Or did you stow away
with a letter to Cousin Jimmy
and a flask in your pocket?

Even if I never know
the port you left from or answers to
all my questions, this I'm sure of—
when I hear the music
that comes out of Noel O'Donoghue's flute,
the sound is so familiar
I swear I have heard it before.

You Could Have Been One

In O'Connor's Pub, music going strong,
Michael Shannon, you could have been one
of the gentlemen guarding their Guinness,
bobbing to the fiddle, tapping hard-soled
shoes on the floor.

You could have been one
leaning in to catch the point of the story;
then, leaning back to laugh,
rosy face to the ceiling,
as if good cheer rises like heat or
smoke out the chimney.

You could have been one of these
if you hadn't had to leave Ireland so young.

Tail of the Celtic Tiger

One could not help but feel justice was accomplished when the Irish began buying real estate in Manhattan during the 80s and 90s. However, with the sobering crash in 2010, those halcyon days ended abruptly. Many young people I met in Ireland had given up looking for work. Some had turned to writing until employment returns. Once again, large numbers are spilling from Ireland's shores.

Bank Holiday Blues

Monday evening on a bank holiday weekend
outside Fitzpatrick's,
where the road turns into town,
young men sit in the waning sunlight,
talking football and lack of work.

Voices amplified by Guinness,
laughter that rings off-key,
faces made ruddy by sun and liquor,
their eyes have travelling in them,
a discontent, a kind of hunger,
not for bread
but for something better than this.

Irish Diaspora

- One million died in the Great Famine of the 1840s, and at least another million of Ireland's citizens emigrated.

- From 1830 to 1914, almost 5 million went to the United States.

- By 1850, the population of New York City was said to be 26 percent Irish.

- An article headlined "Ireland in America" in the *New York Times* on April 2, 1852, recounted the continuing arrivals:

On Sunday last 3,000 emigrants arrived at this port. On Monday there were over 2,000. On Tuesday over 5,000 arrived. On Wednesday the number was over 2,000. Thus, in four days, 12,000 persons were landed for the first time upon American shores. A population greater than that of some of the largest and most flourishing villages of this State was thus added to the City of New York within 96 hours.

- By 1890, 2 of every 5 Irish-born people were living abroad.

- In 2010, 40 million Americans claimed to be wholly or partly of Irish ancestry.

- The Central Statistics Office of Ireland reports the 2010 population of Ireland to be 4.5 million.

A Journey of Discovery

Meeting Tony

Tony appeared our first day in Ireland as if he'd been sent to prepare us for the rest of our stay in his country. I hadn't yet become familiar with the easy way people strike up conversation in an Irish pub, but Tony showed us how it's done.

Curry for Lunch

Tony asks about the heat of the curry,
then like an ebullient bullfrog
he pulls up to my toadstool-size table.
Right off he asks if I have Irish ancestry.
There's something about Tony
that makes me want to tell him all I know
of Michael Shannon, my great-great-grandfather,
an emigrant in the 1840s.

Even the part with shame in it—
how his son, my great-grandfather,
liked his liquor too well.
Such a disgraceful lush he was
that, when he disappeared one night,
no one investigated.
Some suspected his wife, my great-grandmother,
put her brothers up to it.

It's not a pretty story, I say.
*Not the kind of ancestry
one brags about.*
Tony places his hand on mine
as if he were my confessor.
For all you know, he says,
*he may have been a lovely lad
before drink took him over,*
an idea so big it shattered my shame
and anything that separated me
from Ireland.

Tony's Story

The day comes when you've got no
more time left
than you've already spent.
That fact pressed down hard
when I came to forty.
I didn't want to squander
the rest the way I had the first,
on liquor, hard living and trouble.

The only thing I could think of
was to call my aunt Dottie,
the only family member
who would still speak to me.
Come stay here, she offered,
'til you get yourself together.
Her voice so sincere I felt
she meant it.

The room was where
Grandfather Owen had died
just a year before,
his clothes still in the closet.
During the worst of the shivers,
the fearful dreams,
through the delirium, I'd hear,
You can see it through, Son.

Sometimes at night I'd take out
his go-to-church suit and put it on,
sit on the side of the bed
and listen,
You're a good lad, Tony, he'd say.
You just got lost for a while.

Sent Off with Prayers

After our curry bowls have been scraped clean,
Tony takes a dog-eared *Prayers of St. Francis*
out of his coat pocket and insists I accept it.
Our ancestors are always with us, he says.
With the conviction of someone who knows,
he adds, *They will help you if you let them.*
With those words, he sends me off
to meet whatever spirits await me in Ireland.

Presence

By the River Feale,
at Clashmecon,
again at Ballyduff,
at Knockamore and Farranstock,
every day travelling Irish roads,
you are with me.

Sunset, down on the beach
near Doolin Harbor,
surfers—fragile dots, bobbing.
As the water grows dark at sunset,
you hover in the emerging night.

At the park,
sunlight streaming through branches
of a resplendent ash,
a tree ignited.
That brilliant aureole
I took as your blessing.

On a bend in the road
going south toward Dingle,
a young man mowing hay looks up
just in time for our eyes to meet
in recognition.

On the coast, near Ballybunion,
restless high-bred horses
race back and forth, as if to show off
their gorgeous bodies.
I wonder—
Is it in the genes you gave me,
my passion for horses?

If I go to the races
in Galway next Saturday,
Great-Great-Grandfather,
would you be there, too?

I Seem to Remember

Being maidenhair fern,
delicate fans gracing a forest floor.
I lived as a stone, worn smooth by weather.

In the orchard, I sent forth tart apples,
favored for pies, and sour Victoria plums,
perfect for jam spread thick
on fresh-baked scones.

Several springs I came up as
asparagus shoots, in a place
known only to old ladies
who went there to fill their baskets.

I did time as cold, hard metal,
a sword blade forged for battle.

I was an engraved pen
that condemned an innocent man,
acorn on a sessile oak,
satin ribbon tied in a maiden's curls,
hemp sack that transported wool to market.

As a shepherd boy's tin whistle
I piped tunes inspired when, as a lark,
I had sung sweetly in the tall grass of a
meadow.

And so I passed through the years—
glint of dew on delphinium petals,
prey in a falcon's talons,
salmon in the River Shannon.

I was found tucked inside a book of Yeats,
memento of a picnic by Galway Bay,
two lovers long forgotten
except for one dried rose.

Providence

Great-Great-Grandfather,
when you made it onto that boat,
you launched in a direction
that eventually led
to a particular crossroads on the prairie
where your DNA would rendezvous
with the future.

Great-Grandfather, could it be
we are designed
with dreams and needs
that render us mere agents,
moving our species forward
in a universal endeavor?

Grandfather, does it all come down
to the double helix of destiny—
sequence, linkage, spirals,
the trinity that rules?

Mother, was the passion
that led to my birth
merely a new road
drawn on a genetic map?
Your burdened soul, the guilt
that weighed you down,
were they for naught?

Crossing to County Clare

The plan to spend most of our time in one place rather than tour all the counties of Ireland turned out to be an inspired idea. It gave us time to explore, experience and enjoy life in County Clare, a dramatically beautiful part of Ireland.

The Tarbert Ferry

Tern and gulls flirt with a frisky wind.
    I huddle in the bulk of my wool sweater
    to ruminate on questions I carry with me
    like worry beads for times like this.

I wish I could sit just once more
    at my friend's kitchen table.
    We'd have ginger tea amongst geraniums.
    She would have lots to tell me
    about the passage she made just this spring.
    I would listen and learn.

I'd ask, Friend, when you made that crossing,
    did hands reach to help you ashore,
    were the Old Ones waiting there?
    Or was it a dark cave that goes on forever?

In this land of my ancestors, it seems possible
    the Michaels, the Louisas, the Williams
    might send a sign—
    a whisper on the breeze,
    a rune, a dream meant
    to put my pondering to rest.

Perhaps they are saying,
    In good time,
    not now, not yet.

    Don't miss admiring the birds,
    diving against the wind.

So far, my best efforts to research the location of Michael Shannon's home in Ireland have produced nothing beyond the place of his embarkation, Liverpool, 1849. Since I feel such strong resonance with the land and the people of County Clare, I like to think of that part of Ireland as the home of my ancestors. Given that a large number of the Shannons of Ireland call County Clare home, there is some slim logic to my choice.

Leprechauns and Fairies at Work

I don't know why I chose a cottage in Doolin
when there were cottages just as good
in Ballyvaughan or Lisdoonvarna or Kilkee.
Maybe it was that Doolin Harbor
launches ferries to the Aran Islands.
Also, the Cliffs of Moher and The Burren are close by.
Maybe it was its reputation for fine Irish music.
Maybe it was something more.

As it turns out,
every other person in that little town
has the surname Shannon,
many named Michael as well,
same as my great-great-grandfather.
Could it be I was guided to this place?
I'm not usually one for magic,
but this is stranger than fiction.

Thinking of Ireland
Mixed Media Collage

Close to the Edge
Mixed Media Collage

When I had the opportunity to interview N. Scott Momaday, the celebrated Native American author, I asked how he creates the poems and stories he writes about his Kiowa ancestors. His answer could possibly apply to the deep connection I feel to my ancestors. Momaday said: *I think there's a very strong racial memory. Even when you believe that you're imagining something, in many cases you're remembering . . .*

It Depends on What You Mean by *True*

That big boulder in front of our house,
the one I remember the children playing on,
became an icon of happy times.
Years later, coming down Rock Beach Road,
I am stunned to see it was nothing
but a modest lump of limestone.
Memory, that habitual liar.

The mythic missing father
turns out to be a chiropractor from Knoxville, Iowa,
Midwest conservative, Rotarian,
not much interested in lost daughters.
Truth makes fools of us.

Sometimes, in the kitchen or at the sewing machine,
I have the sweet sensation of Mother's approval.
Other times, a dead brother
with a sense of humor makes me smile.
Real and True are tricksters.

Ask the ones who leave crutches and crosses,
pictures of babies, ask them if
the water of Bridget's Well really heals.
Ask and they'll walk away,
pitying you for the question.

My Irish ancestors are with me
on hikes through the hills.
They visit me in a breeze off the ocean.
Even if I make it up, it has a truth
born of longing, my wanting it to be so.

The woman in the gift shop directed me to Michaél Shannon, a resident historian and storyteller who knew more than anyone about the Shannons of County Clare.

Michaél Shannon of Doolin, County Clare

When Michaél Shannon greeted
my husband and me at the door,
I felt like a trick-or-treater come for a handout.
But his warm manner
made us feel at ease right away.

Our host took out clippings of his famous first cousin
William Shannon, journalist for *The New York Times*.
This same cousin had advised Kennedy
during the Cuban Missile Crisis and authored
the noted book *The American Irish*.

Interesting, all of it, but not much could he offer me
except his good wishes on my search
for the place my family came from and agreement
it was like finding a needle in a haystack.

Still, I felt satisfied just to know him,
a man with my ancestors' name,
and to sit on a Shannon sofa in a village that,
who knows, might have been home.

Celtic Roots

On a misty late afternoon,
Michaél Shannon took me to ruins,
some on his own land, just near Doolin.
A long stretch of Celtic treasure
locals walk by any day they like, no signs
to keep anyone out, no warnings to be careful.

Wondrous to see remains of Celtic homes,
a mound where the chieftain would have dwelled,
food-storage tunnels, burial sites,
ceremonial spaces defined by stone walls.

I asked: *Michaél, do you think
your people go back as far as these Celts?*
I do, he declared,
with what I thought to be
a childlike pleasure.

The sureness in his voice
made me decide, until proven otherwise,
the people who lived here
thousands of years ago
would be my people too.

Woman by the Sea

A lone woman, sitting on a ledge by the harbor,
appears to be deep in thought.
Both she and her aged dog look out
toward the Aran Islands
that shine with the low sun's gold.

When I ask about the beehive-shaped
formations just off-shore, she has a ready response,
It's where monks withdrew to pray.
Now only the ruins are left.

Since she seems pleased to have company,
I brave what has been on my mind:
What do you think causes the longing I
and so many others have for Ireland?

Could it be the souls of Ireland's sons and daughters,
cast like spores on foreign soil,
remain unsettled until they come home?

She doesn't respond, but she thoughtfully listens
as I go on: *The phantom pain*
felt by the body that has lost a limb,
might it also occur in those
separated from the land of their birth?

*Could it be my great-great-grandfather's
restless spirit finds in me a way
to walk again on Irish soil?*

*She considers a long time before speaking,
Maybe it's a Celtic knot
that can never be unraveled and best
left alone. Ireland has its way
of casting spells.*

Close Call

Greeting a neighbor on the road into town,
I stepped too far from the edge of the road.
Abruptly, she grabbed my arms
and pulled me forward
just as a car, going much too fast,
screeched its brakes—
missing me by centimeters.

She went on her way
and I turned toward town,
still feeling her strong arms
pulling me toward her,
the grip she had on me,
as if both our lives depended on it.

I felt no need to thank her.
Our eyes exchanged
all that needed to be said—
how in the length of a single breath,
it can be over.

What a strange twist of fate
if my life ended in this place
my ancestor fled!

Driving on the Wrong Side of the Road

At sixteen, there was comfort in believing
everything I needed was in *Rules of the Road,*
a book I knew by heart.

Years later, I find myself driving on the left,
down Irish byways so narrow
hedgerows could take off the mirror.
        Stay left! Look right!
becomes a mantra.
All the rules have changed.

There's a lesson in that:
        When things you've been taught
        don't fit anymore, give them up.

New Rules:
        If I think I have it
        figured out, I look again.

        As I age, black hats and white hats
        become difficult to judge.
        All hats are gray in the dark.

        Two opposing truths, I've learned,
        can each be right.

        Turn over a rock with *anger* on it
        and, most likely, the underside
        reads *fear.*

        Those who survive and live well,
        don't forget, but they come,
        somehow, to forgive.

The road that brings the most happiness
is the one I want to take. I'll follow its rules.

Western Shores

Moody Lion

Some days the Atlantic
laps the west coast of Ireland
like a mother licking her cub,
but no one forgets she can open her jaws and roar.

Cottages and barns, picturesque on seaside hills,
stand ready to confront ocean tantrums.
Battered and bludgeoned through millennia,
these shores have suffered
the tumultuous marriage of land and water.

Crumbling fortresses and towers
that kept lookout for armadas
still stand against ferocious gales,
winds wild enough to level stone buildings,
flip roofs made of tile.

Castles with turrets house ghosts.
Drowned sailors roam The Burren at night,
their voices converging with surf.
Dolmens mark burial places
of those who rise up in flowers.

Changelings

    White stones come unfettered,
        drift up   to float
                like goose-feather pillows.

        Feathers spill
  before morphing into prized lambs,
        lined up   for judges at the fair.
Cirrus puffs keep trying out new acts—
        foam on ale,
    a clothesline of bloomers,
  potatoes whipped fluffy with cream and butter.

    With shifting winds,   clouds step aside
like peasants,
              practiced at sweeping their hats
    in deference to gentry.
              They launch out to sea,
  billowing sails headed   westward
      toward New York or Nova Scotia.

As the sun slumps low
        clouds become heavy,
               turn somber gray,
    the color of loss.

The Great Tree, *Crann Bethadh*

> *Beloved, gaze in thine own heart,*
> *The holy tree is blooming there.*
> — W. B. Yeats

An ancient ash backlit by midday sun—
its branches, its ladders of leaves
outlined in vibrating luminosity,
an aureole setting this tree apart,
saying, *Look, here I am*.

Even now, far from that gravel path,
a tree in Ireland still claims me.
Not the Wise Oak of the Celts,
nor a hazel tree Druids planted at Connla's Well,
nor the Mother Tree
spared in the center of cleared fields.

My own Great Tree,
defining my place in the Grand Matrix,
settling my restless heart.

Huntress

I admire the alabaster cat
who marches past the house each morning,
at least four times, back and forth, patrolling.
This Artemis of the neighborhood,
I suspect, is after mice in the stone wall
by the road.

In four-four time, she steps gingerly
on the macadam, belly swinging
like a hammock on a rolling ship,
a sign of recurring motherhood.

She turns her head to check behind her,
never losing momentum.
She is one of the fortunate ones
who know their calling and
follow it wholeheartedly.
She wears hers as close as white fur.

Early Morning Belongs to Cows and Crows

Guernseys, Jerseys, Holsteins white and black,
an occasional Ayrshire red.
They maneuver the hills, necks stretched
for clusters of grass.
It's hard work gathering enough fuel for a cow.
They're oblivious to the roaring Atlantic
crashing on cliffs below.
Breeching whales give them no bother.
They pay no mind to clouds rolling in
with the look of rain.

They have no interest in Crow,
just landed on a fence
to peruse possibilities,
head bobbing as he does fancy footwork,
side-stepping the thin rail.

On alert for seeds, this indomitable bird
settles for crumbs, anything edible.
He's never heard of cows.

The Town Donkey

Enviable, the donkey who lives
at the corner of the road
into town.

Few go by
without petting his ears,
stroking his neck,
offering a carrot, a biscuit,
a kind word.

The most taciturn townspeople
can't resist
when he comes to the stone wall
to greet them.

He seems to comprehend,
along with the church
and the old schoolhouse,
he holds this town together.

Which makes me think,
not weapons, nor large sums of relief money,
nor better computers,
but things easy to love

like, say, a donkey
might be
what this torn world needs
to knit up its ravels.

Ruminations on Cows

I swear cows pose for my camera,
arranging their silhouettes to best advantage.
I've learned, they are endlessly
shifting position, changing direction,
maneuvering for a more flattering posture.
It's cow ballet in extreme adagio.

Yesterday, five of them in different shades
of butterscotch were scattered about the hillside
when some mysterious command
told them to gather in the shade
of an oak tree next to an old rock wall,
an altogether lovely background for a picture.

Driving the high road,
I looked down upon a dozen
lounging on the crown of a hill.
So like a coffee klatch* I wanted to join in.
But, even with the sound of the ocean
roaring at the bottom of the hill
their only interest seemed to be each other.

Evenings, I've seen them lined up,
both sides of the fence in neighboring fields
as if to confer on the day's news.
A few times, they've turned their soulful eyes
to look me over, then finding me wanting,
gone back to the pleasant harmony
of synchronized chewing.

* For Irish friends unfamiliar with the term, a "coffee klatch" refers to when people, often women, get together over coffee to engage in small talk.

The Burren

The word *burren* is from the Irish *bhoireann*, meaning "a stony place." The Burren of western Ireland is three-hundred square kilometers of landscape made up of gray rock deposited as long ago as the Ice Age. The Burren is especially attractive to botanists in spring and archeologists who go there to study the unique flora and ancient burial sites found only in The Burren.

Along the Craggy Shore

Rough-cut stone slabs, ice-tossed rubble.
Limestone boulders designed
by a master craftsman gone mad,
tumbled terraces, crooked steps,
rock ledges, walls randomly demolished.
And then, surprise!
Out of deep crevices and cracks,
cuckoo flower, dog violet, spring gentian,
bloody crane's bill thriving on bits of seaweed
and dust transformed to meager turf.
White, purple, brilliant blue, magenta,
reprieve of color in this gray-stone,
gray-sky world,
monument to a two-sided god,
Destroyer, Artist Divine.

Beneath the Surface
Mixed Media Collage

Sara's Piece
Mixed Media Collage

The Cliffs of Moher

The Cliffs of Moher stretch along eight kilometers of the shoreline of County Clare. They rise over two hundred meters, presenting a stunning sight and also a danger for those who come too near the cliff edge.

Haunted

Until that sign
I had been enjoying how grasses
and wildflowers on the edge
set off the splendor of water and rock.

Wrapped in five layers of clothes
I had relished the eerie mood—
Manannán Mac Lir's sea breath
rising in mists.

The sign reads,
Want to talk?
a message from the Samaritans
to souls who might
find these cliffs tempting.

That sign—suddenly
I'm on another continent.
A phone ringing in the night
is always bad news.
Until then I hadn't brought
that nightmare to Ireland.

Once again,
those wedded lovers,
beauty and death,
have come to haunt.

The People of County Clare

Brief Encounter

for TED MCCORMAC

He belongs in a ballad—
full white beard,
hair, wind-tousled like a sailor's,
crutch propped against a barstool,
trouser leg folded at the knee.

He leans his head toward
the yarn his bar mate is telling,
one he's doubtless heard before.
All the while, his fingers tap to the rhythm
of the fiddle and guitar.

Later on, after the session
has warmed things up,
he goes forward to sing—
with voice full-throated, strong,
sure of note the way a great tree,
say an oak,
would sound if given a song.

Friday Night at Fitzpatrick's

The flutist dances in his seat,
loose as a puppet
about to be lifted away
to some legendary land
where music is the spoken tongue.
He gasps between long phrases,
pedals floorboards stomped thin
by many nights like this one.

The fiddle player, only nineteen,
with the light above her, a cherub.
She works the strings with delicate fingers.
Hand on the bow, natural as if it were
an appendage. She wears
this music like a second skin.

The guitarist keeps rhythm,
his hand flailing his instrument,
rhythm of hooves drubbing rocky turf,
Epona, Celtic horse goddess,
leading her herd in a spirited romp—
tirump, tirump, tirump.
This may be where it all began,
hammering pulse of the Celtic drum.

The singer sits at the bar drinking his beer,
not looking like a singer at all.
When they wave him up to the mike,
he opens with: *Black, black
is the color of my true love's hair.*
His tremolo makes us believe
he's known this woman.

I love the ground on which she stands,
that plaintive minor mode,
the Irish love.

Fiddle and guitar grow mellow.
He sings—
A time to live, a time to die.
As if a knot had been untangled,
a pensive quiet
wends its way through Fitzpatrick's.

Word Music

Listen to the sounds,
the lilt, the cadence—
whisper of wind over water,
the sheepherder's whistle,
hayforks scraping grass, waves
stroking the hem of cliffs.

Daily gossip is poetry.
They love to talk, these people,
to hear the music of their language,
to taste the Irish words
as they roll off the tongue.

Sounds of a joyful hymn,
sung in spite of sorrow.
Sounds befitting epic tales,
the long story with music in the telling,
a ballad that goes on forever,
persistent, unconquerable.

Fiddle Abstract
Mixed Media Collage

On the Edge
Mixed Media Collage

Milking Time in Winter

For TOMAS MAHON, dairyman of Kinvara, County
Clare and for my stepfather, WARD HOPWOOD,
dairyman of Menard County, Illinois

These Irish cows take me back to Sundays,
the hired man's night off,
when I helped the man I called Father
milk the cows.

It's cold, in spite of heaters.
Hay dust mutes the light.
Barn aromas congeal, sweet-sour, ripe—
freshly washed cement,
disinfectant and cold milk-can metal.

When he slides aside the barn door,
steaming breath precedes hulking phantoms,
one by one in from the dark.
Trump, trump of hooves on concrete.
Colors emerge—black and white, red, amber.

Ponderous eyes, swaying udders;
down the aisle, bodies of bulk and bone
rock single file, peel off
to either side into stalls.

He urges them on: *That-a-way, Sally;*
Step up, Agnes; Good ladies, well done,
more patient and gentle
than I've ever seen him.

He saves out Frieda, the Jersey,
to teach me how to milk by hand.
I can still feel the warm teats,
motion of working down, not pulling,
sound of the rich milk pinging against the pail.

Tomas' cows bring it back,
a side of my stepfather
relaxed and peaceful
I saw only Sundays
when we milked the cows.

Whittling the Day Away

> *Poor the childhood*
> *through which a river does not run.*
> — JOHN B. KEANE

Let's say a young man spends an entire day
whittling a scrap of willow
down by the River Fergus,
His first finger and thumb
move the knife, while his thoughts
wander. No plan to invent
something significant or have an idea
that will save the world.
He just whittles, letting his mind
drift where it will. Then,
when the wood is sleek and smooth,
a lovely replica of a fishing skiff,
he sends it floating with the current
and feels the day well-spent.

Night Coming On

Surfers in Doolin Harbor
on an evening so cold
I wish I had mittens.

Sun poised to slip away,
the evening star already vivid,
they swim out to the island
to catch that last crest of the day.

What it's like to be out there,
I try to imagine.
It must be all about timing,
positioning the feet precisely,
balancing like a fine-tuned scale.

Even the breath, I suppose,
in rhythm with the ocean,
nothing for them except the board
and their body on it.
Maybe the reason they do it—
no time to think at all.

As the water turns deep shades of purple,
shadows engulf their bobbing heads—
they become mere specks,
barely separable from sprays of foam.

I fear for them,
as I do for myself sometimes,
so small, in an ocean of universe,
and night coming on.

A student's notebook I found dropped in a dumpster at the end of the school year became my writing notebook while I was in Ireland. Early versions of many of the poems in this book were written on its unused pages.

Educating Bobby O'Connell

At the top of the page: "Growth by Merging"
and under it a stick-figure skateboarder
with spiked hair and fork-tine fingers.
Evidently Business Class wasn't
fully engaging that day.

But then,
it was April, the height of spring.
Any young man could be forgiven
for not enthusing about corporate mergers
and takeovers.

Essay on: "An invention
that influences our present-day lifestyle."
That page is empty. I want to prompt you.
What about the telly?

You write your favorite show, The Simpsons,
is on every night at six.
Ask your grandparents what it was like
in the Pre-Simpsonian Era.
Did they grow up with ponies and county fairs?
What did they do before television?

Chart of minerals and metals, well done:
bauxite, galena, magnetite.
Good to know what's elemental,
what things are made of.

Drawings of bolts lined up like toadstools
and a page on adhesives and bonding.
Even if you don't use these for mechanics,
you'll need to know what holds things together
as your world grows bigger.

Whole paragraphs of your Gaelic lesson
I translated to get to know you better.
You don't like studying much, but you
do love soccer, play center field.

Bobby O'Connell, you are a good lad,
I can tell. I'm writing this poem
on the blank pages of your notebook
and almost falling in love with you
as I write it.

"John Player's cigarettes."
Oh, my, they've already gotten to you!

For Religion Class you wrote, "People
believe that once you die you go to a place
called heaven." My dear Bobby,
I wonder what you believe.

Now that it's summer
I hope you're fishing some river
or skateboarding,
letting your own truth emerge
from the green hills.

Siochán leat, peace be with you,
I looked up how to say it in Gaelic.
Shee-oh-con-lat, Bobby O'Connell,
peace be with you.

        A slightly different version of this poem
        appeared in *New Mexico Poetry Review,*
        Spring, 2011.

Irish in America

"Farmed Out"

When my great-grandfather Michael Shannon left my great-grandmother Louisa Martha McKinney Shannon penniless, she was forced to place some of her children in foster care. Ed and Will, ages ten and eleven, were "farmed out," as they said in those days, placed on two separate farms to live in the barn and work for keep.

My grandfather Will told the story of his first placement with a heartless man who put him to work cutting timber for coal mine shafts. One day when the farmer and my grandfather were working down by the river, a neighboring woman passed by. Not seeing the boy, she asked the farmer where he was. "Oh, he's over in the tent feeling poorly," the man answered.

When the woman went to check, she found Grandfather with a raging fever. Horrified by the boy's condition, she hurried home to prepare remedies which she gave him each day until he improved. Without her help, it is almost certain he would not have survived.

As soon as he was strong enough, Grandfather escaped that farmer and headed toward the place where his brother Ed was living. Walking miles, travelling mostly between corn rows for fear of getting caught and taken back, he finally found his brother. After telling his story, he was settled at a neighboring farm with a more caring family where he stayed until he was eighteen and free to go out on his own.

* * *

That the child Will who received such sparse education (only up to fifth grade) and such little support or affection could have turned out to be the responsible, loving adult that Grandfather Shannon became is a marvel. Often, when I would tell someone I was Will Shannon's granddaughter, the response would be, *Fine man, Will Shannon*. And a fine man he was.

Beloved

for my Great-Grandfather • 1851-1888

Some people suspected murder
when Michael Shannon was found
in a neighbor's field over by Sugar Grove.
However it happened,
it was really drink that killed him.

It might have seemed nobody cared,
especially my great-grandmother Martha Louisa
who remarried soon after.
I doubt anyone thought to ask
the two little boys and the little girl
what they felt
about their daddy being dead.

For drink and trouble he was infamous.
No count was what they called him.
But you have to wonder—
somewhere in Ireland
was there someone news of this death
would sadden?

On a narrow road
in a lime-washed cottage,
was there an aunt, an uncle, a cousin?
Was there someone
who got a letter and mourned
that drink had taken another?

Scriofa i Rúnda (Written in Secret)
Mixed Media Collage

Irish in America
Mixed Media Collage

A Snake Still Lives in Ireland

It's hard to find a place to park
in this rosy-cheeked town
on a sunny Saturday morning.

If I hadn't entered a dim-lit pub
to inquire which way to the bank,
I might have passed over the rest of the story—
Saturday morning drinkers lined up at the bar,
each studying his pint, reverently,
as if it were a caldron, a potion,
a sacrament.

Just like the night before,
except, now, no fiddle nor banjo,
no jigs nor reels, no drinks on the house.
These are the devoted.
They look up with suspicion
while the bartender gives directions.
I am an invader in this tribe's territory.

If I hadn't stopped in a dim-lit pub
on a sunny Saturday morning,
I might not have witnessed the underbelly
of the snake that still lives in Ireland.
The snake that killed my brother.

Martha Louisa McKinney Shannon

for my Great-Grandmother • 1856-1915

1)

Grimly she stirs a pot of thin soup
while Edward, William and Etta play
in the small main room of the clapboard house.
Their father Michael won't be home 'til long after dark,
drink being his one true love.

As she stirs, a plot forms, an end to waiting and
worrying, never knowing when the next row will start.
Jaw set taut, she's a she-wolf
who will fight her way out of this trap.

2)

One night, when he doesn't make it home at all,
not a tear is shed.

Rumor has it one of her brothers
was seen soon after
wearing the dead man's watch.

3)

Martha Louisa—
four husbands, a passel of kids,
some let out for keep too young,
I look at your picture and wonder
if you were as tough as they say.

Only if I tie the strings of your apron
on myself and imagine a houseful of youngsters,
no money in the coffee can,
and a husband who's a drunk, only then,
can I embrace your grit and thank you
for the small measure that has come down to me,
a streak of resolve that has served me well
more than once.

Men in Gray Suits and Hats

A sea of gray suits surges through
the streets of Dublin, an Irish political rally
photographed circa 1930.
Serious-faced Irishmen, stern for the cause.

Under those hats, it's the face of my grandfather
over and over—
prominent nose, lofty forehead,
sharp-boned cheeks.

Under those hats, worried eyes
witness to all they have borne.
My uncle had those eyes, gray-blue.
The only son, responsible
for whatever went wrong.

My grandfather's eyes, brown eddies,
his whole story in them, a gentle heart
and the will to stare trouble down.

Gray suits, gray hats everywhere in Ireland.
In a County Kerry town, mourners mingle
on the sidewalk when a funeral lets out.
Talk out front after is part of the ritual.
It reassures them they're not dead.

Ladies in black, men in gray suits, hat in hand.
Shoulders of the tall men recall
Grandfather's straight back.
I hear him telling me, as he often did:
No matter what, remember
to stand straight and tall.

William Michael Shannon
Ready for a Sunday Drive • 1940s

photo by Herbert Shannon

Grandfather at 50

Mid-1940s • Athens, Illinois

It is Sunday.
You can tell by the hat and suit,
the Sunday way he holds his shoulders,
shiny shoe on the running board
of the '39 Ford.

Hat brim conceals his eyes,
puts his prominent nose,
his sharp cheek bones in shadow,
but his mouth is braving a cautious smile
because the coal mine pays well,
better than all those years of plowing,
laying railroad ties and driving mules.

It took plenty of Lava soap last night
to get the soot off
but now he has finished
a grand fried chicken dinner
with cherry pie for dessert.
His family is waiting to take a drive
but first, the camera.

He's come a long way for this picture,
from the shed behind the barn
where he bedded down at ten
after being turned over
to a farmer to work for his keep.
He's hammered, shoveled
grunted and sweated
all the way to this Sunday—
possibly the best of his whole life.

Previously appeared in *Tender Harvest*
published by Black Swan Editions, 2009

Lunch Time for a Gandy Dancer*

                Second generation Irish in America

After a morning of hammers striking spikes,
silence and shade are blessings.
His black lunchbox waits—
sandwiches of leftover meatloaf, homemade pickles,
two apples, tart and firm the way he likes them,
chocolate cake, spread thick with frosting.

It's the rich chocolate cake that awakens
reverie of another lunch break over by Tallula
when he was a hired hand at the Kramer place.
Home for lunch, children off to school—
heat curling his wife's hair at the temples,
salty taste of skin, fingernails digging into his back.

That was before typhoid almost took Martha the eldest,
before the 1918 flu,
before at least a dozen farm jobs,
one move after another,
before dollar-a-day wages,
before too much trouble wore his wife down.

Now, he's proud to be getting better pay.
He likes railroad work, the rhythm he gets into,
his muscles coming down hard with each blow.
He takes pleasure where he can get it—

      * *Gandy dancer* is a name given to those who
        drive spikes in building and repairing track
        on the railroad.

coffee still hot in the thermos,
a round of checkers with Shorty or
a foursome of cards if Mike and Joe are up for it.

Then the whistle.
Taking up the hammer again, he recalls—
the spirited horse he saved up for
with money in a coffee can
and then had to let go
when times turned hard again.
That handsome mare he saw only once later,
harnessed to a plow.
He strikes the first spike square.

Mining for Coal

> Eddy Coal Company, 1939 • Athens, Illinois

Seen from afar—they could be dutiful ants, queued up
with their treasure of crumbs;

closer—identical black lunch boxes, carbon headlamps,
belts hung heavy with gear;

closer still—hands, spread broad by hammer, chisel, shovel;
deep-lined faces, scrubbed clean of yesterday's dust.

Look how these men lean in toward each other;
coal has made brothers of them;

hear them laugh at old jokes, forgetting for a moment
the big chunk of life spent underground;

listen as they are called—Eddie Brown, Mugs Jankowski,
Shorty Abel, Will Shannon.

Watch as the elevator opens and they descend into the dark.

William Michael Shannon
Ready for Work • 1930s

photo by Martha Shannon

Inheritance

Long nose, big ears, strong back—
these come down to us from the Irish.

Hoeing, raising chickens, driving mules,
picking cherries, shoveling coal—
Grandfather did it all,
an overtime work ethic he passed on.

My mother needed to keep her hands busy
with crochet, embroidery, quilting.
Maybe she got that from the Irish.
I'm quite sure it was the knitting I got,
the need to keep needles clicking
whenever I sit still, to keep those
I love in sweaters.

We Shannons
are honest as the day is long.
Uncle Herbert was the only mechanic
people would trust with their cars.

We are storytellers—Grandfather,
who passed on lore of the old days;
his son, Uncle Herbert, who loved
to tell droll jokes and tales
he'd picked up along the way;
and I who put mine in poetry.

Until I went to Ireland, I had no idea
there was an entire island
where people liked to talk
as much as I do.

Alcohol too got on the boat,
passed through Ellis Island
and took up residence
in America.

In the small town where I grew up it was customary to ask children the question: *Who are you?* It meant: *What is your lineage? To which of the resident families do you belong?* That question might have made me feel awkward and unworthy since I carried a name not known in those parts, the name of a father I never knew. Fortunately, I was saved by being able to say with pride: "I'm Will Shannon's granddaughter."

What's in a Name?

I am Will Shannon's granddaughter.
I am the hero in an ancient tale told
beside a fire after dark. I am also
the villain, the fool, the horse.
Every ballad, every rousing song
has me somewhere in it.

A strain of fierceness runs in my veins,
blood of painted warriors and fiery women.
I vibrate with the beat of the bodhram,
both struggle and survival in it.

My clan defies border and time,
part English, part Irish,
part oppressor, part oppressed.
I am mongrelled,
two sides of any coin.

I am the riddle of the intricate knot,
a string of baubles, many-colored,
more verb than noun, still becoming.

I am the child who looks out through
the gate, waiting; I am the mother
who comes to fetch her home;
I am the father whose ship never returns.

I am every child who wants to know
to whom she belongs, her true name.

I am Will Shannon's granddaughter.

POSTSCRIPT

Someone's Always Saying Goodbye*

1)

747s lift whole villages into the clouds.
Day and night, summer, winter,
wingéd vessels transport
rows and rows of stories into thin air.
Across continents and oceans
dreams vaporize into jet trails.
Like migrating cranes,
giant silver birds take flight,
leaving those who stay put,
suspecting everyone they love
plots to fly away soon.

2)

Neil leaves day after tomorrow
to visit his son in San Francisco.
He's proud his boy married Irish,
happy for his prosperity in The States,
but nights he lies awake
trying to recall the shape of his son's face.

Every few years Mary from the bookstore
visits her brother Brian in New York.
He's done well with his own deli
in a ritzy neighborhood.
He tries to coerce her to come
work in the business. She says,
Maybe someday, but Mary knows
she's not one ever to leave Ireland.

A Tralee construction worker
has been without work
two years. Other downturns
he went to France or Germany, even
Australia once. But bad times
have hit there too. For now,
he's writing poetry and playing guitar,
ready to leave in a minute
if he hears of work. Anywhere.

3)

So it goes—in a country where
loved ones are strewn
like a broken string of pearls,
where everyone seems to be
somewhere else.

At first I was sure a mist of grief
must hang over this land, but
there's no proof of it.
The Irish may know something
about love I've yet to learn.

Perhaps it is my need
to keep everyone I love close
that makes me want to sweep up
all Ireland's scattered children
and bring them home.

* Title from a song by VEHNEE SATURNO & TITO CAYAMANDA,
made popular by ANNE MURRAY

In Appreciation . . .

to those on both sides of the Atlantic who helped bring this book to fruition:

MARSHA AHRENKIEL, my daughter-in-law, brought her artistic flair and considerable talent to designing this second book we've done together.

HARRY CLIFTON, Professor of Poetry for Ireland, graciously gave his attention to the manuscript.

MARIAH HEGARTY, gifted poet and editor, helped shape these poems into a book.

LYNN HOLM, faithful editor, sought out every last wayward comma and suggested the final order of poems.

JOAN MCBREEN, notable Irish poet, read the manuscript and gave astute feedback.

JAMES MCGRATH, poet-friend, urged me to attend Writers' Week in Listowel, County Kerry and, thus, set me on this path.

JOHN MCGRATH, teacher, poet, and Listowel friend, blessed the book with his words and tutored me on correct Irish spelling and pronunciations.

Lillie Morris made this project a delight by sharing her enthusiasm for Ireland and by embellishing the pages with her beautiful art.

Etain O'Malley saved me from some of the cultural missteps I might have taken.

The Praise Poets' Group gently nudged me toward better poems.

Micháel Shannon of Doolin, County Clare, enriched the book with his stories and lessons on Irish history.

Robert Wilber, my beloved, saw me through this and all other projects with patience and good cheer.

Lillie Morris

About the Artist

Georgia artist Lillie Morris works primarily in mixed media collage, enjoying the creative freedom it allows. Her artwork is included in many private and corporate collections and has been shown in exhibitions throughout the Southeast as well as during Writers' Week in Listowel, County Kerry, Ireland.

Her intense interest in Ireland has taken her there numerous times, especially to Listowel, which she considers her Irish "hometown." She has enjoyed two residencies at Cill Rialaig Artist Retreat near Ballingskelligs, Co. Kerry. (2006, 2009)

In addition to her artwork, Lillie enjoys playing traditional Irish music. Her classical training on the violin, which began in her childhood, equipped her to embrace the Irish fiddling tradition when the music captured her heart in the late 1990s. Since that time she has studied with some of today's most highly regarded Irish fiddlers and performs in the Augusta area. When in Ireland she enjoys playing in sessions with Irish musicians.

Lillie and her husband Bill reside on a farm near Appling, GA. She is represented in Augusta by the Art on Broad Gallery.

http://www.lilliemorrisfineart.com
http://lilliemorriscollage.blogspot.com

Linda Whittenberg

About the Author

Linda Whittenberg's childhood in small-town Illinois stamped her with midwestern ways inseparable from her as person and as writer. She admits it takes only an hour or so of being with kin to slip into speech patterns and intonations that grow right out of Illinois soil.

The American West and its landscape, particularly the mountains and deserts of New Mexico, captured her heart almost four decades ago when she first made her home in Santa Fe. She and her husband Robert Wilber live in a rural setting where they are currently companions to a mule, a goat, and two cattle dogs.

Linda Whittenberg's earlier books, *Tender Harvest* and *Dying Can Wait*, reflect both her Illinois and New Mexico roots, as well as years of mothering, teaching and serving as Unitarian Universalist minister. More recently, with visits to Ireland, she has discovered another place of deep, soulful resonance. As Irish writer Joan McBreen commented: *I would say that at a psychic level Ireland has probably always been your first country! How come it took so long for you to get here?*

http://www.lindawhittenberg.com